Pebble®

I DON'T BULLY

I Am Fair

by Melissa Higgins

Consulting Editor: Gail Saunders-Smith, PhD

Content Consultant: Susan M. Swearer, PhD
Professor of School Psychology and Licensed
Psychologist; Co-Director, Bullying Research Network
University of Nebraska–Lincoln

T0052258

CAPSTONE PRESS
a capstone imprint

Pebble Books are published by Capstone Press,
1710 Roe Crest Drive, North Mankato, Minnesota 56003
www.capstonepub.com

Copyright © 2014 by Capstone Press, a Capstone imprint. All rights reserved.
No part of this publication may be reproduced in whole or in part, or stored in a retrieval system, or transmitted in any form or by any means, electronic, mechanical, photocopying, recording, or otherwise, without written permission of the publisher.

Library of Congress Cataloging-in-Publication Data
Higgins, Melissa, 1953–
I am fair / by Melissa Higgins.
pages cm.—(Pebble books. I don't bully)
Summary: "Simple text and full color photographs describe how to be fair, not a bully"—Provided by publisher.
Includes bibliographical references and index.
Audience: Age 5–8.
Audience: K to grade 3.
ISBN 978-1-4765-4069-6 (library binding)
ISBN 978-1-4765-5173-9 (paperback)
ISBN 978-1-4765-6038-0 (ebook pdf)
1. Fairness—Juvenile literature. I. Title.
BJ1533.F2H54 2014
179'.9—dc23 2013029995

Note to Parents and Teachers

The I Don't Bully set supports national curriculum standards for social studies related to people and cultures. This book describes being fair. The images support early readers in understanding the text. The repetition of words and phrases helps early readers learn new words. This book also introduces early readers to subject-specific vocabulary words, which are defined in the Glossary section. Early readers may need assistance to read some words and to use the Table of Contents, Glossary, Read More, Internet Sites, and Index sections of the book.

Printed in the United States 5961

Table of Contents

I Play by the Rules 5
I Am Open Minded 13
I Treat People the Same 17
Everyone Deserves a Chance 21

Glossary 22
Read More 23
Internet Sites 23
Index 24

12
16
Wilson

I Play by the Rules

I treat everyone
the same way.
I'm fair.
I don't bully!

I play by the rules.
Kids who bully only care
about winning.

I wait and take my turn.
Kids who bully push
others out of the way.

I share with everyone.
Kids who bully
leave others out.

I Am Open Minded

I see different sides of a problem. Kids who bully don't think about other people's feelings.

I listen to everyone.
Kids who bully
don't care what others
have to say.

I Treat People the Same

I try to treat everyone in the same way. Kids who bully pick favorites.

If a bully is being
unfair to me,
I stand up for myself.

Everyone Deserves a Chance

Being fair means everyone can play and be heard. No one deserves to be bullied!

Glossary

bully—to be mean to someone else over and over again

deserve—to have a right to something

equally—in the same way

fair—in an equal way